P9-CMX-775

Science Matters

SCREWS

Michael De Medeiros

WEIGL PUBLISHERS INC.

Published by Weigl Publishers Inc.
350 5th Avenue, Suite 3304, PMB 6G
New York, NY USA 10118-0069
Website: www.weigl.com

Library of Congress Cataloging-in-Publication Data

De Medeiros, Michael.
Screws / Michael De Medeiros.
p. cm. -- (Science matters)
Includes index.
ISBN 978-1-60596-039-5 (hard cover : alk. paper) -- ISBN 978-1-60596-040-1 (soft cover : alk. paper)
1. Screws--Juvenile literature. I. Title.
TJ1338.D37 2009
621.8'82--dc22

2009001941

Printed in China
1 2 3 4 5 6 7 8 9 13 12 11 10 09

Editor Nick Winnick
Design and Layout Terry Paulhus

Photograph Credits

Weigl acknowledges Getty Images as one of its primary image suppliers for this title.

Contents

What is a Screw?

Screws can be found all around you. They are used in furniture, drills, garage doors, and some musical instruments. Many people keep small screws around the house to use in building projects.

Screws are tube-shaped tools with sharp edges called **threads** spiralling around them. They are often used to fasten objects together, such as metal, stone, and wood.

■ Screws are one of six simple machines. People use simple machines to make daily tasks easier.

How do Screws Work?

Screws convert movement in a circle to movement straight ahead.

Imagine twisting a screw into a block of wood. With a screwdriver, you can get a good grip and turn the screw. When you turn the handle, the threads twist toward the wood block. Since the threads are at an angle, turning the screw pulls it into the block of wood. The **shaft** of the screw stays in one place as the handle turns.

Thanks to the angle of the threads, the screw can change the twisting **motion** into a straight-ahead motion. This moves the screw forward. It may take many twists to move the screw just a little way. Turning the handle the other way will lift the screw out of the wood block.

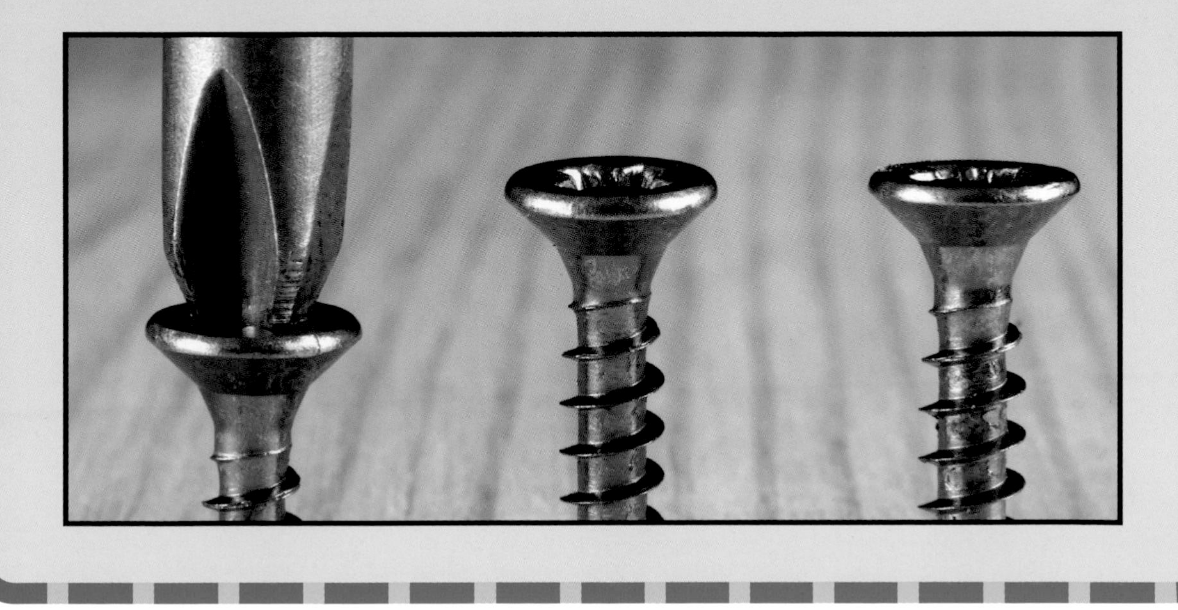

Sharp Threads

The threads on a screw can be widely spaced or narrow. The angle of the threads can vary. They may be quite steep or very shallow. In machines that make use of screws, the threads can be many times wider than the center part of the screw.

■ Threads on a screw need to have a constant angle and even spacing to work well.

Following Threads

Think of the threads of a screw as a ramp that twists around the shaft.

As a screw turns, the threads dig into an object, such as a block of wood. Keep turning, and the screw moves deeper. You can think of it as the block of wood moving up the ramp of the threads.

The threads are evenly spaced. Each time the screw is turned, it ends up in the same place it started. However, it is now one thread deeper in the block of wood.

You can predict how many turns it will take to twist the screw all the way in by counting how many threads it has. You can measure the space between threads to see how far a screw will move with each turn.

Pushing Ahead

Screws perform a difficult task. Fastening screws push their way into solid objects. Drills slice holes in materials such as metal and stone. This requires a great deal of **force**.

Screws work because they move at a slow and steady pace. A screw with a many threads must be turned many times to twist all the way into an object, but each twist will require less force. This is known as the **mechanical advantage** of the screw.

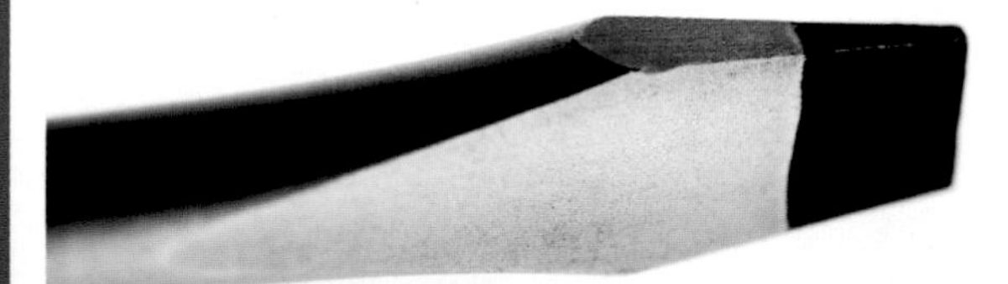

■ Some screwdrivers have a star-shaped tip, while others are flat. The tip must match the head of the screw.

Overcoming Friction

Friction is a force that occurs when two objects rub against each other. It keeps objects from sliding smoothly. Rougher objects produce more friction.

Most parts of a screw rub against the object it is twisting into. This produces a large amount of friction, even if the object is fairly smooth. Screws use their large mechanical advantage to move without being stopped by friction.

Friction can be helpful when using screws. Screws are often used to put wooden furniture together. They make strong joints because friction holds them in place. This gives a screw an advantage over a nail.

Nails do not have threads. This means there is less friction holding it in place. Nails are more likely to loosen than screws.

Screwy Gears

Gears are wheels with sharp spikes around the edges. They lock together with spikes on the edge of other gears. When one gear turns, the spikes press on the spikes of another gear. As a result, the gears move together at the same time.

Worm gears are shaped like screws. The threads act like teeth. When the worm gear turns, it turns the gear that connects to it. This provides a great deal of power. It can also change the direction that the gears are moving.

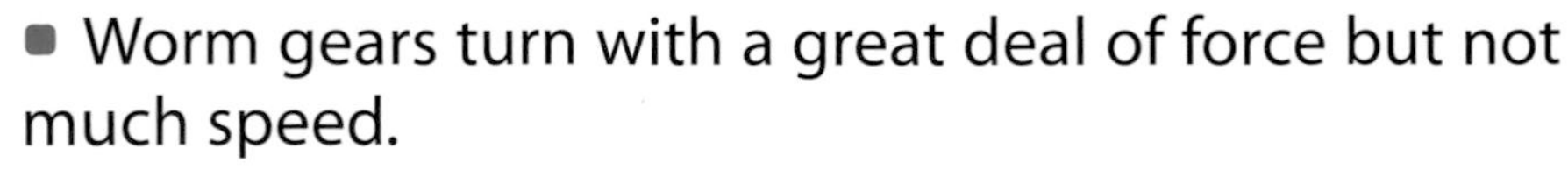

■ Worm gears turn with a great deal of force but not much speed.

Where is the Worm?

Worm gears can be found in many places.

Garage Door

Many garage doors use a worm gear to raise and lower. These doors can be very heavy. The slow, steady motion of a worm gear keeps the door motor from working too hard all at once.

Double Bass

Musicians who play a double bass use worm gears every time they play. The strings of a double bass need to be twisted very tightly to be **tuned**. Worm gears are used to stretch the strings. The mechanical advantage of the worm gear makes this easy on the musician's hands.

Nuts and Bolts

A bolt is a type of screw with a flat tip. Bolts are often used with nuts. A nut is a small metal ring with a pattern of grooves. These grooves are a perfect match to the threads of the nut. Nuts are screwed onto bolts to hold them in place.

Bolts are useful for joining objects that may need to be taken apart later. Bolts turn more easily than screws and are less likely to loosen or fall out.

- Bolts come in many shapes and sizes.

Benefits of Bolts

Car Parts

Many parts of the body and engine of a car are held in place with bolts. One car part can wear out before another. For this reason, bolts are useful because they can be removed easily.

Furniture

Bolts often are used instead of screws to make furniture joints stronger. A bolt is less likely to loosen under pressure than a screw. This is useful for items, such as beds and couches, that may need to hold many people at one time.

Temporary Structures

Bleachers are temporary seats that are used at concerts or sporting events. Scaffolding is a set of ramps and platforms that lets workers build high above the ground. These often are put together with bolts so they can be put up and taken down quickly.

Drilling Bits

A drill bit can act as a screw. The edges of the threads on a drill bit are sharpened to cut the material it twists through.

Most drills are turned by motors. They use a great deal of power. The drill bit turns very fast and is pressed into the material to be cut. As the cutting edge of the drill bit turns, it carves out a hole the size of the drill bit.

- Drills are important tools in metalworking, construction, and manufacturing.

Diverse Drills

Every craftsperson or builder lives by the saying, "the right tool for the right job." There are many different types of drill bits, each used for a different job.

Stone

Masonry

Metal

Wood

Early Screws

Early screws were used as pumps to transport water from low levels to higher levels. A large screw was placed in a long tube. The bottom of the screw was placed in a lake or stream. As the screw turned, water became trapped in the threads. The water was then pushed upward. After a few turns, the water would pour out the top of the tube.

The screws that we use today are a recent invention. Standard sizes for screw threads were only created during World War II.

■ Being able to raise water uphill using screw pumps meant people could water crops without waiting for rain.

The Hanging Gardens

Two ancient scientists came up with the idea for the screw pump. One was a Greek named Archimedes. The other was King Nebuchadnezzar II of Babylon.

The king's wife was from **Persia**. She missed the lush plants that grew there. The king built the Hanging Gardens of Babylon to grow the same types of plants that grew in Persia. Nebuchadnezzar used screw pumps to carry water up to the plants in the hanging gardens.

Gaining an Advantage

There are six simple machines. They are ***inclined planes***, ***levers***, ***pulleys***, ***screws***, ***wedges***, and the ***wheel and axle***. All simple machines are designed to make work easier. These machines do not have batteries or motors. They do not add any **energy** of their own to help people do work. So, how do simple machines work?

Simple machines work by changing the forces that are applied to them. In most cases, they do this by changing the distance or direction of a force.

Inclined Planes

Inclined planes are sloping surfaces that connect a lower level to a higher level or the opposite.

Lever

A lever is a moveable bar that rests on a solid point called the fulcrum.

Pulley

A pulley is a wheel with a groove around the outside edge. In this groove, there is a rope or cable. Pulling the rope turns the wheel.

Screw

Screws are tube-shaped tools with sharp edges spiralling around them. They are often used to fasten objects together.

Wedge

A wedge is a triangle-shaped tool with a sharp edge. It can separate two objects, lift an object, or hold an object in place.

Wheel and Axle

Wheels are circle-shaped objects that rotate around their center. They often have an axle in the middle to hold them in place.

Surfing Simple Machines

How can I find more information about wedges and other simple machines?

- Libraries have many interesting books about simple machines.
- Science centers can help you learn more about force, motion, and friction through hands-on experiments.
- The Internet offers some great websites dedicated to simple machines.

Where can I find a good reference website to learn more about screws?

Encarta Homepage
www.encarta.com

- Type any term related to simple machines into the search engine. Some terms to try include "screw" and "mechanical advantage."

Science in Action

Screw Origins
Many inventions are created by using old ideas in new ways. This exercise shows how screws work.

You will need:

- paper and scissors
- a colored felt marker
- a pencil and a ruler
- scotch tape

1. Use your ruler to draw a triangle on the paper. Be sure the triangle has one **right angle**.
2. Cut out the triangle with your scissors.
3. Draw a line along the longest edge of the triangle with your marker.
4. Attach the shortest side of the triangle to the pencil.
5. Wrap the triangle tightly around the pencil. Observe the shape of the line you drew when you have wrapped the triangle all the way around the pencil.

What Have You Learned?

1. What is a screw?

2. What does a worm gear do?

3. What is used to turn a fastening screw?

4. Where did King Nebuchadnezzar build the Hanging Gardens?

5. Why do drill bits cut material instead of fastening it?

6 What were early screws used for?

7 What is one reason bolts might be used instead of screws?

8 How can you tell how many turns a screw will take to be twisted into an object?

9 Which force must screws overcome in order to turn?

10 Does a screw with many threads have a greater mechanical advantage than one with few threads?

Answers: 1. Screws are tube-shaped tools with sharp edges called threads spiralling around them. **2.** A worm gear provides a great deal of power and can change the direction gears are moving. **3.** A screwdriver **4.** In Babylon **5.** Drill bits have a sharp edge at the end of their threads. **6.** Moving water to higher levels **7.** Objects built with bolts can be easily taken apart again. **8.** By counting its threads **9.** Friction **10.** Yes

Words to Know

energy: power needed to do work

force: the pushing or pulling on an object

friction: what happens when two surfaces come together

mechanical advantage: the amount of force needed to make something move or work

motion: movement of an object

Persia: the country now known as Iran

right angle: corner of a square formed where two lines meet

shaft: a long, narrow rod

threads: ridges along the outer edge

tuned: fixed an instrument so that it played the correct notes

Index